CW01081669

FOR THE MESSENGERS

Jude Cowan was born in Manchester and lives in London. She is a historian, archivist and songwriter. *For the Messengers* is her first collection of poetry.

FOR THE MESSENGERS

Jude Cowan

Donut Press

Published by Donut Press in 2011.

Donut Press, PO Box 45093,
London, N4 1UZ.
www.donutpress.co.uk

Printed by Aldgate Press,
3 Gunthorpe Street, London, E1 7RQ.

ISBN: 9780956644510

A CIP record for this book is available
from the British Library.

in memoriam Fadel Shanaah (1984-2008)

ACKNOWLEDGEMENTS

Acknowledgements are due to the editors of *Cartys Poetry Journal* (www.cartyspoetryjournal.webs.com), *Pen Pusher Magazine and Writers' Hub* (www.writershub.co.uk), in which some of these poems first appeared. I would also like to thank Andy Ching, A.B. Jackson and Liam Relph for their efforts in shaping this collection for publication.

At the request of his family I have used the anglicised surname Shanaah when referring to the late Palestinian journalist Fadel Shanaah. Shana and Shana'a have been other commonly used spellings.

CONTENTS

PREFACE

I began working with the Reuters archive by accident. While completing a PhD in film history I'd taken a job on Newsfilm Online for the British Universities Film and Video Council. The project's aim was to make over 3,000 news stories available to educational subscribers, utilising the collections at ITN Source. This included items held by ITN for Reuters Television. Before the project was completed, however, I was invited to join the team which operates the 'Reuters Desk'.

The world I entered demanded engagement with intriguing, challenging, often upsetting video material; I was cataloguing and researching for a huge, world renowned news agency. Footage arrived each evening on large Digibeta tapes, and at the end of a shift one of the team would pick up the day's selection from the reception desk.

I quickly orientated myself, becoming aware of the different 'feeds': News, Sport, Showbiz and the quirky Life! I'd never seen unpackaged news like this; these were simple edits, free from imposed commentary and far from the polished broadcast news bulletins of British television. My daily viewing now included content such as the immediate aftermath of disasters and bombings, messages produced by paramilitary groups, and even executions. It felt a natural step to try to process my response to the work by writing; and poetry, for me, was the best medium.

My writing quickly became a habit, almost a compulsion, quite possibly a therapy. By the time I showed a sample to Andy Ching, the editor at Donut Press, I'd collected a large number of poems. He suggested that I continue throughout the calendar year, 2008. We could then assess whether what I'd produced would be worth publishing.

This target helped me to stay motivated, but as the weeks passed a series of dilemmas became apparent. First I noticed that certain slants had begun to appear in the way some countries were represented.

Others were conspicuous by their absence. When I reviewed the footage we received it was clear this tendency was already present. For example, coverage was very strong in terms of Middle East stories, with gripping first-hand accounts arriving from operators working tirelessly in Gaza, Jerusalem and Israel. It was impossible not to connect with the passion of these camera teams and what they witnessed. By contrast, pieces from India were mostly created by the Indian television network ANI and were bought to form part of the Life! feed, which provides material equivalent to the And Finally slot of ITN news bulletins.

The reason for this is, of course, commerce. Despite its size and considerable ambition, the Thomson Reuters agency cannot cover every news event around the globe, and commercial demand prompts the provision of a constant flow of generic items. I quickly decided my work should reflect these realities and I became more aware of the recurring journalistic tropes – preparation, aftermath, conference, presser, interview, protest, funeral – and more conscious of the role played by selection and editing. At points I've drawn attention to these conventions in my poems. Following poets (such as Fred Voss) who write about work, I have at times contextualised my writing within the day to day archiving environment. Hopefully this will help to highlight the way in which scenes were mediated before my witness: each story arrives at the archive after a complex journey, helped on its way by camera operator, journalist, producer, editor, also input desk operator and courier.

Sustaining a lively level of writing through the year proved far from easy. It was necessary to explore a number of strategies to help keep my response as fresh as possible. I sought inspiration from diverse poetries, often hunting down authors who had written about conflict and upheaval, especially on an international scale: the First World War soldier poets and those, like Czeslaw Milosz, who experienced the Second World War as civilians; writers working in the shadow of holocaust, notably Paul Celan; and the Palestinian poet Mahmoud Darwish, whose work I only discovered after Reuters covered his death on 9th August 2008.

While initially I found myself drawn to the sense of immediacy offered by free verse, as the year progressed I began to experiment with popular traditions and historical genres such as the epigram, nursery rhyme, folk song, and also the mystical text of Christopher Smart. Perhaps this gives an effect of striving towards a gentle Brechtian distantiation, although this only occurs to me in retrospect. The quantity of work I had to produce thankfully left too little time to reflect on the scale of the task, or to immediately assess the quality of my achievement.

Looking back, it occurs to me that if 2008 hadn't selected itself by chance, it could have been chosen for its salient characteristics. During these months the international landscape shifted and huge cracks opened in global capitalism. Early economic confidence in the finance sector was replaced by September crash, and by October the International Monetary Fund was warning of systemic meltdown. Lifestyle choices were questioned, the glitter of ostentatious glamour started to flake away to reveal DIY and green-centred issues. In the USA the end of the presidency of George W. Bush and the election of Barack Obama gave hope around the world that there would be change. There were also the first Olympic Games to be held in China, the conflict in Georgia and a number of huge natural disasters. A diverting exercise in hindsight is to see how some events which later grabbed international headlines were pre-shadowed – the social unrest in Greece springs to mind.

Despite the mental pressure necessitated by the project, since its completion I have sensed a loss in my daily routine. My concentration has slipped down a gear, while emotional reactions have been tempered. To me this shift testifies how poetry increases engagement. The act of writing led me to look closer, go deeper and connect more strongly. And it encouraged a more intense appreciation of the work of those who, equipped with camera and microphone, have gone into the most difficult and dangerous situations to bring back impressions of what it's like to live in extremity. Some journalists, like Fadel Shanaah, tragically killed in Gaza on 16th April 2008 at the age of twenty-four, have given their lives because they believed in the power of such storytelling. This book is dedicated to them.

Jude Cowan

FOR THE MESSENGERS

MEXICO: WARLOCK

The Brujo Mayor wears yellow to attract money.
He turns his tarot to the Empress.
Hillary Clinton will be the next US President.

Prediction bursts through ruddy cheeks,
springs from ebullient eyebrows,
trickles down his long grey beard.

He grows serious, tells, country by country,
of a terrible series of disasters.
Central America will almost disappear.

Acolytes cast spells. Journalists scribble.
A good day's work, another quirky tale
captured for the Reuters Life! feed.

SYRIA: GOLAN HEIGHTS

The capital was returned
intact but changed.
It had learned to conceal

secret places which held
the power to alter even
the most humdrum of lives.

We found that these radical,
shattering spaces might be
uncovered at any moment.

Walking along the ashen road,
a door may suddenly open
on an alternative existence.

A person, unaware, can seek out
these transformational spots
in unassuming, idle moments;

one must always be vigilant.
When the mind reaches
for a new toy, the body is not

far behind, stretching out sinewy
yet vulnerable limbs. So, I think
I understand. When you had

a break from learning
you thought you'd wander a short way
from the school gates? Two metres?

Well it was far enough for you
to lose your fingers, picking up
that 'pen'. Let that be a lesson.

The doctor says everyone
has feelings of loss.
Also, fingers are overrated.

RUSSIA: HEALTHY EDUCATION

Marina Danilicheva pours cold water
over a boy at the Rosinka Daycare Centre.
He rolls around the snow in his underpants.
She still swims outside at sixty-five:
We are doing it to get strong, not weak.
Shoppers go past wrapped up in overcoats.
The children run barefoot on powdered streets.
One prefers food and warmth, she backs away
from the bucket. Inside, they're climbing
a rope ladder, jumping, doing forward rolls
on the rug, swinging from rings. Two girls
are framed by rotting, peeling paintwork.
A ripped paper snowflake is stuck to the window.

SAUDI ARABIA: OIL HUNTERS

Before the oil we were shepherds
and drivers of camels, chasing stars,

crossing unmarked borders. Beneath
the wide tent we drank-in quiet,

our teapots nestled in roasting charcoal.
Then came oil. Wellheads bloomed, their

metal trunks withstanding desert heat,
growing strong on rich calories of black blood.

Riyadh teems with petrol pumps, and down
its streets we shunt in mighty machines,

managed by signs directing our migrations.
Transparent parabolas praise the cliff

of Kingdom Tower, water plays
like children at its palm-strewn feet.

INDONESIA: SUHARTO

Shadows of the *Wayang Kulit*
shiver on his cotton screen,
give a final shudder
and dissipate into the *dunia*.

With his close family in the room
the great *dalang* slips away,
1.10 p.m., Sunday 27th January 2008,
with multiple organ failure.

Java's motorbikes throb.
Man in t-shirt: *His death is natural.*
He and his cronies destroyed Indonesia.

Woman in headscarf: *He was a good man,*
God will give him a good place.

Young man in white *kopiah*: *He's dead.*
We don't need to argue about him any more.

Secure in an office, KontraS speaks
for the disappeared and victims of violence.
We cannot forget the past.
Other bereaved need justice.

An Iman prays, *May Allah pardon his sins.*
A worshipper cycles into the mosque courtyard:
He'd been in power for thirty years.
I don't know much about his politics.

UNITED KINGDOM: BILAWAL BHUTTO

In the Great Quadrangle at Christ Church,
saluting the sky with a black and white brolly,
over the mowed lawns he comes – her son,
the boy we expect to be next.

He walks the rain-washed flags, turning
his profile right and left, calmly obeying
journalists' requests. The rain can be
persistent in Oxford during January.

IRAQ: SIFTING

In Salhiya a woman goes
back into the rubble
to collect her paraffin heater.
It's needed even more without walls.

BOLIVIA: ALASITA FESTIVAL

Prayer is infinitestimal
and can dance
on the head of a pin,
yet craves infinity.

Models are minute
compared to
their real world
signifieds.

Jan Feb Mar
Apr May Jun
Jul Aug Sep
Oct Nov Dec.

This poem prays
to Ekeko,
the tiny god
of abundance.

KOSOVO: NEW COUNTRY

February 17th. A new country struggles
to wake with espresso, paper and cigarette,
preparing for work on the worn, claret seats
of Tricky Dick's Café. In the first light
the waiter flicks on the generator –
chugging against expected power cuts.

INDIA: COSMETIC SURGERY

I have seen the businessman,
    sporting sweat bandana,
        cycling to nowhere,

the thrusting professional proving
    he can raise and lower dumb-bells
        and travel the conveyor belt;

observed the male model reclining
    with Bollywood mag in salon chair,
        styled, waxed and quiffed;

doctors overalled in green, lowering scalpels,
    cutting the relaxed belly, removing fat,
        stitching back skin.

The Image Consultant sucks his lips,
    advises a young metrosexual how
        to correct his gynecomastia.

USA: SNACK

$175 House Special.
Cows fed beer and sake,
massaged daily.
Coarsely ground flesh,
chopped black truffles,
Gruyere aged in Swiss caves,
hon shemeji mushrooms
garnished with gold leaf.
Winners on Wall Street
celebrate with a hamburger.

UNITED NATIONS: COUNCIL

Punctuating speeches with the rhythm
of the written word, editors cut
United Nations conference stories

with inserts of the eternal biro
scratching letters onto
a spiral-bound notepad.

The strawberry-sleeved scribe
practises her calligraphy:
schedule, schedule, schedule.

When coming generations peruse
this identic commentary in their
post-apocalyptic archive of erstwhile video

poets will prize the editors' iconic iterations
as a profound lament for meaningful purpose,
a prescient vision of Earth's hollow years.

IRAQ: SUICIDE BOMBER

It's a puzzle. Did she give herself
voluntarily for suicide?
She's only thirteen (US soldiers think)
and when she decided she wanted
to understand fourteen and even
higher numbers, she gave herself
to the police, who removed
her explosive vest.
                          A woman she
didn't know approached her
with the device, then helped her put it on.
Covered by a blanket, Raniya talks
about the why and who and how,
taking the backwards and forwards steps
of question and answer, marking out
the dialectic, the basic mathematic of living.

USA: MEAL

Two pepper jack
barbecue burgers
with crispy onions,

baked potatoes
with sour cream,
bacon and cheese,

a large
strawberry
milkshake.

All finished off
with a cocktail
of three

lethal drugs,
courtesy
of the state of Georgia.

NORTHERN GAZA: REMAINS

The red crescent moon arrives
in the remains of the day. It remains
to adjust the covers, lift and push
the tray into the morgue refrigerator.

Some friends remain outside the gates.
The stocky man in orange and red
checked shirt uses a mobile phone
to tell his family all that remains.

SYRIA: ARVAD

And the inhabitants of Sidon and Arvad
were thy rowers: Ezekiel remembered
the ancient republic, fair island city-state,

tonguing his cruel thoughts into ashen bitterness,
visioning Tyrian merchants sinking into ruin,
abased and bald. From this sun-cradled port,

curious traders and warriors went east for spices,
west for tin, carrying Baal, Yam
and Mot, and spreading this alpha-bet:

A was an ox,
                B was a house,
                                M water.

COMOROS: STABILISATION

Stabilisation of the island is crucial. That's why
we deploy these men. This interview is to tell you
how important it is that our operation goes
smoothly. Sitting in this office in this heat
isn't easy. See the reports, ring-bound behind
my head, and the way my skin glistens. I wear
this suit to stop me sticking to the chair; this
isn't a room for mistakes. We have to control
the situation, secure the other islands.
The people must, above all, be careful,
and we are preparing advice on how to behave.

KAZAKHSTAN: SPACE PROGRAM

Leafless birch point skyward
outside the Baikonur Cosmodrome.

One day before blast-off, Yi and her
Russian colleagues (sitting in quarantine
behind the glass) are asked to recall
the journey which brought them
to this concrete building in the forest.

The nanotechnologist crayons
trains travelling in space. Volkov thinks
of his father on Mir, looking down
on the end of the Soviet Union.

Red and blue logos promote
scientific dreams of clarity, organisation,
enterprise and peace.

Thumbs up from Yi. *Enjoy our flight.*

SUDAN: STREETS

Despite the curfew, some still walk
the red earth lanes of Omdurman.
The wind is picking up plastic bags
and branches, bringing too much motion.
Across scrubland, storms approach.

EGYPT: IRAQI EXPATS

See this huge catfish? I've pulled him
straight from the roadside tank.
I balance him by the gills.

He gasps. Such a healthy,
dying struggle stirs the appetite.
Imagine the tasty Masgouf this one

will make when he's opened
along his belly,
squashed flat between hot grills.

Hear his skin sizzle, car horns hoot
in Cairo's grid-locked suburbs.
Wash him down with fizzy Vimto,

then we're off to the billiard hall
to pot balls while chatting
on how we live in this great city…

       … when all the while we're
circling Baghdad's dry fountain,
round, round, going round,

hoping that clever Kahramana
will take pity on our longing
and fill our empty jars.

USA: LONG ISLAND

Approaching fifty, Cathy is pleased
she and her fiancé can afford to buy
a foreclosed white clapboard property.
The estate agent's bus regularly tours
these monuments of domestic distress.
High heels tack up stairs past olive-painted
walls. The child investigates cupboards
for stories that may have been left behind.

IRAQ: ANNIVERSARY

Night-time explosions
on the Baghdad skyline.

A soldier sleeps beneath
a 'Baghdad or Bust' gun turret.

Saddam comes toppling
off his plinth. The girls and boys

aboard the Abraham Lincoln
look a bit pink as they clap

Bush's revelation
that the US has prevailed.

The politicians are getting steamed;
their big day fast approaching.

And so the fifth anniversary
is marked in this beautiful rotunda.

IRAQ: SHOTLISTING

We can sell this pool footage
of the aftermath of a car bomb.
Shotlist: smouldering wreckage
covered with debris, blood, etc.

Most of it is okay to show on our website
but we must tag images of boys
sitting 'round in wet soot
as *Children Identifiable*.

NEPAL: NEW YEAR FESTIVAL

Dolphins. A sea of dolphins leaping.
The turmeric prow plunges deep into the crowd,
crest catching arrows of the sun.

The tremendous street-ship lumbers
and lists. The deity's men smile, rocked
so comfortably on the shoulders of chaos.

Walls and roofs shakily support spectators,
craning necks to see the chariot roll,
perhaps tip over. Chattering gulls circle,

snatch dropped morsels that litter the wake
of the gods' progress. Giant wooden wheels rotate
into evening. Oil lamps bless the willing ropes that tow

the heavy spirit house up the hill. Fortune settles, rests,
flutters on the churning sea of live faith which ebbs
and flows in these vertiginous, piercing mountains.

WEST BANK: OPERATION IN JENIN

The residents are bringing flowers
for the soldiers. Palestinian police
and the Presidential Guard arrive.

They begin performing drills.
There's a spring in their 'column left' march,
their 'inclines', even their 'at ease'.

The commander comes
to talk to our journalist
about Operation Smile and Hope.

He hopes Israel will be more
co-operative than last year.

JAPAN: FERTILITY

A big pink penis wobbles, wiggles, born aloft
by worshippers at the Kanamara Matsuri.

Suckers of penis lollipops perform to the camera,
such erotic confections lubricating counterfeit intimacy.

Prayers are offered for protection against HIV,
for boyfriends and babies: traditionally

that's what girls think about during spring –
that and cherry blossom.

USA: PRIMARIES

Stopped in the street
on the way to work:
does he think
it's time for a woman
to take charge?

He shakes his head,
wrinkles his brow,
shakes his head again –
shaking the idea
from his face
like a dog shaking
water droplets
from its coat, chilled
after an unexpected dunk.

I think that Hillary,
for one reason or another,
is just divisive.

He throws back his head,
expelling the last
remnants of this
unpleasant possibility.

BELGIUM: FALCONS

Michel and Gudule are raising their kids;
their wide wingspans shelter four chicks.
He brings home rats, small birds and pigeons
which she lovingly prepares. This couple
eked out a scrape high in the cathedral.
Their clutch was warmed by her powerful body.
Huddled around their caring mother, each day
her creamy-down darlings grow bolder,
calling for food from the safety of home.
Workers abandon tasteless office lunches
to witness this model of family values,
these few days before the proud parents push
their large-footed young out from the tower.

GAZA: REUTERS CAMERAMAN

5 p.m., Wednesday 16th April 2008.
Fields shimmer in sunlight.
Fadel aims his camera
across the valley at a tank.

Flash, smoke, shell, then
sudden dark.
The mic picks up a crunch.

A frantic camera.
Two boys and a torn bicycle
lie on the road.
Further on, the spot where
Fadel lies with his friends –
still, strangely twisted.

Someone removes
his damaged camera.
His 'TV' car rages,
spews black smoke.
Its side is split, back
blown off. Flechettes have
perforated its windscreen.
The soundtrack now
is screaming.

At hospital, Fadel is greeted
by his chief mourner:
t-shirt drenched in family blood,
he cradles his dead brother.
Someone dangles
the camera with its broken lens.

A photograph: Fadel stands
before the Dome of the Rock,
supports his camera on his shoulder.
Bright creamy skin, dark gaze,
pensive fingers. Such long nails.
Did he play guitar?

Someone else holds the camera.

LATVIA: SOVIET ERA EXHIBITION

Everyone is to be included. People must be painted
with great precision. In realism, daily life
will be ideal. In the Soviet Union it is always sunny.

A list of advisable themes will include:–
1. Communist construction. 2. Working class heroes.
3. Happy childhood. 4. Well-being of Soviet society.

Exhibitions will be organised according to Soviet festivities:–
1. Anniversary of the Revolution.
2. Commemoration of the life of Lenin.

So she painted:–
1. The goodness of hay.
2. A father gesturing to his pigtailed daughter.
3. All they surveyed from the communal tractor.
4. Village patriarchs viewing society from the
   perspective of pre-annexation.
5. Folk dancers in Abrene costume.
6. Tuba players blowing spiritual notes.
7. A cup used for toasting the Satversme.
8. Feet that had walked through the Great Depression.
9. Hands that held Latvian hands.

CHILE / ARGENTINA: VOLCANO

Grey snow has fallen this May
in Futaleufú and Esquel.
This garden rose could have come
from Miss Haversham's dusty boudoir.

No wonder that dog stays close
to the farmer as he gathers hay.
When allowed outside, a child must cover
her nose and mouth with a damp bandana.

An old man trudges the street,
glares down at his feet, kicks up
small clouds as he goes.
This May, grey snow has fallen.

GERMANY: FRITZL

The (ex) friend is reading newspapers
in the orchard. The blossom's in focus,
he's indistinct – red and white blurring
into pointillist pink – but we know who
he's talking about. The *Bild* shows
'Das Inzest-Monster' reclining
on a sun-lounger in red swimming trunks.

There was a lot that didn't add up,
the (ex) friend explains.
He bought a dress in Thailand
that wouldn't fit his wife. He loved
Tom and Jerry and when it was on
he couldn't stop laughing. The (ex) friend
didn't know he had such a large basement.

MYANMAR: CYCLONE 1

Today is not the day to sit
at a lakeside restaurant,
sipping Singha beer
while noodling with a shrimp dish.

Even the Royal Lake is being lifted
and blown away, high
above buildings and falling palms.

The world's weather –
wind and water – is passing over
very quickly, taking with it
the breath of Yangon.

MYANMAR: CYCLONE 2

In Myanmar, people are answering
questions with their own words.
This is something we haven't heard
for a long time. What is the occasion

of this sudden change? Three days ago
Cyclone Nargis ripped apart Yangon.
What is Myanmar going to do now?
Is anyone going to answer that?

GREECE: STRIKE

Do not imagine this is any strike.
This is our strike against a return
to medieval working conditions.
To reduce public debt (what is that?)
the government plans to sell stakes
in state-run businesses. Once the
greed is slaked comes the hunger.
Do not imagine this is any strike.

IRAQ: SADR CITY TRUCE

Who will guarantee tomorrow
in our dusty alleyways?
Ceasefire moments only borrow
from the violence and the graves.

GAZA: CROSSING

The border at Rafah
is open again
and we will go to Egypt.

Bring your papers
and bring your pain,
we will cross to Egypt.

The wearied and worried,
the wounded and weak,
ready to go to Egypt.

The medical workers
are waiting in green,
waiting for us in Egypt.

May God make us
whole again,
we are going to Egypt.

CHINA: EARTHQUAKE

Don't say I'm pessimistic,
I know what I'm thinking,
watching water gush
from the bottom of the dam.

Folks pass me by, negotiate
cracked roads, ford broken rivers.
Shadows lengthen over operations,
fresh waves of troops

are dispatched,
which helps to lift the gloom.
How to organize? This effort
isn't helping my angina.

Tools and wishes are spread
on cloth to keep scalpels, tongs
and bandages clean. Carried in
every backpack, solutions and futures.

CHINA: AFTERSHOCK

In this sorry season
we wind through a valley
of vegetables, thoughts
far away from farming.

I want to walk backwards,
carrying this baggage,
balanced on my back,
reversing time

to before the Fall.
Losing my parents
I have found
the full meaning of Paradise.

UKRAINE / HUNGARY: BORDER

Along the tree-fringed, water-routed edges
of the European Union a speedboat chases down
smugglers and smuggled; night-vision binoculars
watch for border contraventions, dogs are at the ready.

Crime syndicates have bamboozled hope, grown richer
on innocence. Men have made many journeys
to become detainees in camps, playing cards
behind barbs, drying trousers on the wire.

FRANCE: CANNES FESTIVAL JUDGE

Cigarette.

When somebody operates
without a brain
and without a heart
they kill hundreds of thousands of people
around the world.

Another cigarette.

The inane stupidity,
the lack of good.
Films are about love.
The brain has a purpose
in connecting to the heart.

Offering a cigarette.

It is a shame
that we have to bastardise
the term politics
by attributing it to people
like George Bush.

Lights a cigarette for a French actress.

RUSSIA: BICYCLE PROTEST

The naked cyclist is showing off his pecs,
demanding bicycle lanes and respect
from St Petersburg drivers.

He rides in circles over the cobbles,
his tyres bouncing vivaciously
up and down on Winter Palace Square.

JAPAN: G8

After Edward Lear and Thomas Love Peacock

Stepping ashore at the Terrible Zone:
Q: State, exactly, what is your interest.
A: Butcher. Baker. Candlestick maker.

G's eight wise men we be
and we sail away in a sieve.
Though the sky be dark and the year be long
we'll never think we're terribly wrong;
and we promise you this, while economies live,
it won't be us that will get upset –
no, we won't get wet.

CHINA: OLYMPIC WEDDINGS

We will get married on 'fa' date,
so our lives will be far better than

they were for our fathers.
The bride will dazzle, not fart.

We will have millions of farthings,
be so lucky, so fortunate, favoured

by fat number eight. Our queue
for wealth will win the farthest race.

Signed:
Mr & Mrs
08-08-08

UNITED NATIONS: NORTH KOREA NEGOTIATIONS

All parties agreed
that the declaration
was subjected to verifications,
and there is agreement
within the parties
on a set of principles
to guide the establishment
of a verification regime.

Meanwhile, there is agreement
to establish a supervising
regime to supervise
the implementation
of the commitments
made by all parties.
All parties reiterated
the aim in a verifiable way.

UZBEKISTAN: KARIMOV

How wonderful
to see you again,
Mr President. Do

take this bunch
of red roses.
Shall we dance?

In a land-locked spin
we waltz in gold
and cotton

while the pale
moon rises
on the promise

of oil and gas
in the Aral Sea,
and the promise of

our ten million young
learning to love
their nation's

beauty and terror.
So, Mr Karimov,
shall we dance?

PAKISTAN: MOUNTAIN CEREMONY

The crowd have gathered by the riverbank.
Expectant faces turn towards the performance.

Stewards wield swords. The two Afghans
accused of spying for the US military

squat blindfold beneath a protective grove
of guns held by selected guardians, each

honoured to be a mighty tree of fire,
as the executioner prepares his tools.

NEPAL: FIRST GOVERNMENT

King Janak was the father of Sita,
goddess of virtue. King Mahendra
thought such lives too Indian
for his 'one nation, one culture'.

King Gyanendra did not listen
to Hindu tales in which
our worst enemies are reborn
as our children, fulfilling karma.

A plain man from the lowlands
of Janakpur walks to the podium.
This first president is the son
of a peasant, and a Madhesi.

BOLIVIA: INDIGENOUS INDUSTRY

Bruno keeps around 300 llamas.
He makes fires from their dung,
sells excess meat
which is increasingly in demand
as dehydrated jerky or vacuum-packed steaks.

Vicuña run across the plain,
are herded into corrals,
wrestled to the floor and sheared.
In the factory, workers wind wool
and shake out red cloth in bright waves.

A designer has been seduced by camelids.
She arranges the clothes in her boutique:
A great inspiration for my creations.

SERBIA: ARREST

What happened to the trim locks
and smart suits in which this leader
told attentive soldiers
how to make enemies and eradicate people?
Can eleven years on the run change a man?

His beard and hair grown long and wild,
sprouting freely in video and newsprint.
His two-faced two faces roam Europe's media,
encapsulating Karadžić past and present,
professional dispenser of war and medicine.

He shall receive our finest justice.
As seconds shift, angry observers watch
for the minutest of changes
in his concentrated face.

Light clouds play on his wrinkles.
He makes a tiny turn of the mouth,
brings a slight quiver to his eyes.

The doctors aren't sure
if this ocular treatment
gives relief of any kind,
but he must drink his medicine in public.
He must be seen to take it.

VARIOUS: KARADŽIĆ

The former US Ambassador said
they will transfer Radovan to the Hague
and let him become part of the slow

but effectual war crimes tribunals.
This was clear. Why did I think he said
Let him become part of the show?

EGYPT: SURVEY

Guide to Everyday Street Life for Women.

Expect:
1. Ogling.
2. Touching.
3. Shouting of sexually explicit remarks.
4. Exposure of genitals.

Because:
a. *You ask for it, with your provocative, seductive clothes.*
b. *Girls want to be harassed these days*
   (the last girl he flirted with hit him).
c. Worsening economic and social conditions.
d. Lack of awareness of true religious values.

Despite belief to the contrary, apparently
wearing a headscarf makes no difference.

JAPAN: BELLY FESTIVAL

Whose face would you create with your stomach?
Which alter-ego would glare at fascinated children
from your nipple eyes? Whose mouth would bellow
from your navel as you crab-dance, zig-zagging
the tarmac, chanting *Wassa matter, eh?* Perhaps
your tummy has always secretly harboured a wish
to grind and whine like Madonna? Come on ego,
make a cartoon of yourself – purify your essence,
release your repressed selves. Just for an afternoon,
indulge those patient alternative personalities who
stalk the corridors of your inner house. I saw one
just then (it was Pikachu!). For Art's sake,
naturalism is not the only performance.

CHINA: OLYMPIC COUNTDOWN

Astonished,
gathered 'round
the clock,
tallying times:

minutes marked,
seconds split,
doors blasted
open,
    riven,
struckapart.

Smiling, cheering,
head bands,
flags –
minds on fire.

Security keep
dissidents
far away;

choreography,
inside
and outside
the Bird's Nest.

Boom and prosper:
we will thrive,

flourish.

Ten nine, go!

seven six,

down to

zero.

GEORGIA: GORI UNDER BOMBARDMENT

Framed by a blown-out window
the masters continue their war games.
Black knight to d3. White king to f3.
Consult the almanac.

The cabinets were falling.
I ran over here. Then a bomb hit
the military base and we hit
the wall; but I'm still alive.

Bishop takes rook. Check.
Big countries always play
with little countries
and crush them as they choose.

Unlike chess, it's not
a game of wit, but of force.

BELGIUM: NATO GEORGIA STATEMENT

The door that locks away the past
can not be opened. It must be opened.

Leave your weapons at the gate, pass
swiftly through the time portal, squeeze

the impossible *djinn* back into his pickle jar
and return to the *status quo ante*.

CHINA: OLYMPIAN YELENA ISINBAYEVA

She already has the name for her future perfume.
A scent for the strong, determined woman,
not the glamour girlie who's like a baby.

Her passion is pumped by high-as-the-sky adrenaline.
She breathes in belief before she flies above the bar.

Her tight jeans, glittering Dolce and Gabbana belt.
I consider the range of this former Russian army officer.
I'd buy her essence if I could bear cologne.

ZIMBABWE: NEW PARLIAMENT

The smell of shit on the streets
goes up the noses of MPs
and judges who cheerfully parade
a new season of power.

The old government is refreshed in Zim,
where nightmares about zeros
harry bankers, and money is printed
with an expiry date.

When you're riding through hell
you just keep on riding, scream
the four horsemen,
hooves churning the red earth.

AFGHANISTAN: MEDALLIST RETURNS

Due to the intermittent power supply
many couldn't watch the taekwondo bout

in which he won bronze for the nation,
but his victory was replayed over and over

on local stations. Rohullah comes home
to a hero's welcome and a house,

awarded by the president. He sees
his medal as a message of peace.

USA: NOMINATION PREPS

Signs for each State are suspended.
Young women polish steps to a lemon fresh
sheen. On-stage screens show
Stars and Stripes flapping in the breeze.
Balloons rise and bob on the ceiling while
the techie checks that the gavel's rap
will ring clear across the Union.

UNITED KINGDOM: HBOS PURCHASE – A CEO SPEAKS

'This is one of those extraordinary times
when all is uncertain. We have seen
an enormous amount of liquidity dry up
and impacts are ricocheting through
a desiccated framework. Our combined
banks will have an unrivalled reach.
Creative people backed by solid capital
will innovate. A competitive high street
will benefit consumers enormously.'

KENYA: RIFT VALLEY SNOWFALL

White cold has drifted onto the hillside and surprised the maize.
Young men wear snow like hats, taste the stuff, flip flakes like
confetti. They're out for a stroll, pushing bikes and leaving tracks
through the covered grass, making an unfamiliar crunch. Hands
cup crystals, bring frozen water sensation to interested bodies.
Screaming teens snowball fight with this thin, unexpected layer,
generously donated by the valley's patron: a changeable blue sky.

USA: MULTI-BILLION DOLLAR RESCUE

Troubled assets need relief;
it's clear as mud and twice as deep.
Dig Peter's pockets to pay Paulson,
fund our finance institutions.
Everyone must shove a bit,
to roll our system out of shit.

LIBYA: GADDAFI / RICE

Too much history, too many set-tos,
too much bad feeling, too much past
that isn't past enough to allow his flesh
to touch hers. They didn't shake hands.
We all saw it. He meant us to.

UNITED KINGDOM: MRS BROWN

When she sees that clouds brew sinister,
she goes before him to the sinners:
My husband and your prime minister.
And through her eyes they see a winner.

FINLAND: VIGIL

"I was next to where the guy was, in the next class. I didn't know what was going on when he was shooting. I was just like 'oh well, someone is just kidding' and then, after a few minutes, one of my classmates went outside to check what he was doing, and he was like going to shoot them and they ran away. I still didn't know what was going on, I was still in the classroom and then a few minutes later one of my friends came into the class and she was so scared. She just didn't know what was going on, so we had to hide under the table so we'd be safe somewhere, because we didn't know what was going on, if he would be coming into our class or what was going on."

"I am so scared and don't know what to do ... I thought this is a safe area. I've been living here all my life. It's a small town and safe but I don't know if it's safe anymore."

IRAQ: FUNERAL

The child puffed, and he blew
the condolences tent, himself
and twenty-five others
all the way into the next world.

RUSSIA: DAGESTAN WEAPONS

The overturned truck spills militants, guns
and army backpacks through half-open doors

and onto the road channeling the olive-green
northern slopes. It's cold in the shade

and the grey-haired security officer wears
an anorak over his uniform; but despite

the temperature he seems satisfied
with this up-ended haul. It's an important one,

with so many young men drifting over
borders into guerrilla warfare.

AUSTRIA: HAIDER

after Christopher Smart

For I will consider the chief, Haider

For he has crashed his black sedan before the Klagenfurt dawn

For a politician he received adoration both fervent and fanatic

For he was a sun-tanned man of action and friend of
    Arnold Schwarzenegger

For he moved through life in sprees of energetic motion

For he enjoyed roller-blading, bungee-jumping and marathon running

For he was dramatic by nature and a passionate actor

For his fiftieth birthday he hired a mountain, was dropped on the summit
    by helicopter and skied down to eat a giant *apfel strudel*

For he described SS officers as 'upstanding men of character'
    (although he later recanted)

For we were never sure just how much he was a neo-Nazi

For he was a friend of Saddam Hussein

For he drunkenly hit a concrete barrier and rolled and rolled and rolled

For we suspect not all the cats in his bag were killed

For they loved him and light altars in the restaurants of Carinthia

CANADA: BEETLE

He flicks the bark off with his bowie knife
and there she is, right there, chewing
on the bare pine. She's tiny – size of
a grain of rice. Chomping and changing
fifteen million hectares of British Columbia –
changing the ecosystem wholesale.

USA: McCAIN

What is the matter with Mr McCain?
He's crying with all his might and main
that he feels all of America's pain.
What is the matter with Mr McCain?

What is the matter with Mr McCain?
You'd think he was under enormous strain.
He's promising jobs and tax cuts again.
What is the matter with Mr McCain?

What is the matter with Mr McCain?
Has the economy put a worm in his brain?
He doesn't like money being poured down the drain.
Perhaps that's the matter with Mr McCain?

What is the matter with Mr McCain?
Don't let him tell his Nam story again,
there's twenty days left of his bloody campaign.
Best keep on talking, old Mr McCain.

AFGHANISTAN: ABDULLAH WARDAK

Outside Kabul
there's a blown up,
flipped over car,
and the Governor
of Logar,
his bodyguards
and driver,
like the car,
have bodies they can
no longer use.

AFGHANISTAN: AID WORKER'S FUNERAL

Dear diary, if anything happens to me –
like being shot anonymously
while walking in daylight under
pale blue and mutable clouds –
I want to be buried in Kabul,
where I have spent my best hours.

I've been allowed to give precious minutes
to its children. I have been overpowered
with the joy of sharing. Life ends
and we sleep, a fate that awaits
the most vital reader, who may
even now be leafing these pages.

On my special day there will be guitar hymns
and the scent of flowers. Mother and sister
will shower rose petals on my final box.
I'll appreciate your goodbye gifts
and forgive motorcyclists who ride on,
sputtering, through the sunlit, backstreet labyrinth.

UNKNOWN LOCATION: MILITANT VIDEO

Copyright: <u>SUICIDE BOMBER AMATEUR VIDEO</u>

Note: *** Re-use with caution as this is not Reuters copyright.

No resale without filmmaker permission. ***

FRANCE: STRIKE

Dockers aren't children, they are men, real men,
and if we have to show it, we will show it.
A docker bares his arse at the tear gas.

EGYPT: CHEOPS' BOAT

In the base of the Great Pyramid,
under stones piled with the greatest
deliberation, there is a sealed pit.

Inside sits a pristine boat, primed
for sail. When called by Ra, Pharoah
will be set to hoist his colours.

If Apophis (the crocodile of chaos)
damages the sun god's raft, morning
could be delayed. Perhaps then Cheops

could step in, offer him his cedar craft.
This ghostly fleet of pharaohs travel
the netherworld through roots of trees,
passing underfoot like tube trains.

IRAQ: CHANGE

The lads are crafting video messages
of congratulation. They do this well,
for soldiers are used to making
animated postcards
to bolster the spirit of absent family.

And in this victory aftermath
these young men stand
for a more wholesome everyman,
being one step removed
from the thick of our economy.

They occupy a territory more
black and white than our dull
grey skies. One suntanned marine
has a serious point
which he's eager to share.

This election has given him hope
that you can accomplish anything,
no matter what your race, colour
or creed. His words don't sound tired
but ring fresh with belief.

INDIA: OBEROI HOTEL VIGIL

You, dear girl, are hands on mouth,
sad, biting, picking, nervous.

You, lady, are standing staring,
your heart filled with family.

You, old man, old friend, old chap,
you are here – we can hold you!

You, son, are on the phone, to let
home know. You'll fill eyes with tears.

You, government man, tell us how
we will be more prepared, next time.

You, world, watch with us –
prepare yourselves.

INDIA: MUMBAI RELEASE

Grateful to the rescuing forces,
three lucky hotel guests roll suitcases
over questions and into taxis.

Three more re-borns, their
first cries over, take pleasure
in lungfuls of street air.

UKRAINE: YUSHCHENKO

He is careful. He has good reason to be.
His pocked face shows he is a survivor,
though only just. He swallows before
speech, knows the importance of words
and is determined to make them count –
every one. He is an expressive, passionate
man and his gestures are decisive, but
they are contained – movements made
under close scrutiny. When his words
cease, his lips press tight, waiting for
a greater pressure to come. And it will
come, it has come before and will come
again. Again there will be everything
to play for and he will play as hard,
as hard as he must. He knows he must.

ITALY: KERCHER CASE

Corridors and briefcases.
Reproductions of inoffensive art
in perspex frames. Smoking,
waiting for procedure to take
its long course. In and out
of municipal rooms, heels clacking.
The victim's family find out
what has to be done for justice.

IRAN: ANIMAL SHELTER

Dog-keeping has been denounced
as Western, un-Islamic and unclean.
Anyone who walks their pet outside

can be fined. Dogs in public places
can be impounded. Volunteers vaccinate,
neuter, groom. A trail of dog food

is drizzled 'round the pound.
The kennel gates are opened.
Cats sit in columns of colour:
            white,
            ginger,
            black.
Multi-furs crowd bowls.
This is controversial charity.

AUSTRALIA: LIFE SALE

Second-hand life for sale:
kitchen, jetski and spa.
Friends included with the house,
plus a trial job in a rug shop.

Holding a beer he grins
from his hammock.
Optimistic faces are pulled,
papers signed.

HAITI: PEACEKEEPER

You can't see his body
where it lies in the truck. Perched
on the roof, photographers capture

a final likeness. Quiet eyes under
azure and cobalt helmets
wish this trip uneventful,

in view of the last, when,
delivering food in uniform, their colleague
was dragged from a car and shot.

USA: NEW ORGAN

Take pale red chambers
of collagen, fibronectin
and lamnin. Wash clean.
Pack with immature cells,
gorge on nutrient-rich
fluid. Attach pump, apply
pressure, stimulate. In
eight days, heart beats.

GERMANY: ZOO CHRISTMAS

Long sun bear claws pull away red-gold giftwrap
taped with festive care to a cardboard box that,
we may imagine, the keeper has saved specially
since her microwave arrived. A sloth bear

has grabbed a gaily-papered tube, can sniff out
stuffed innards flavoured with syrup. Slowly, snout
dipping beneath the seal of angels, he sucks up
so many concealed, congealed, termite treats.

Two cold, firm hands clasp the shins of a small boy
who cranes above his father's head. Today
he rides this shoulder car to learn
how beautifully bears unpack presents.

UNITED KINGDOM: SURVIVAL

Living on after the big boat has washed her,
flotsam, into the armchair of a retirement home,
Miss Millvina Dean, sweetheart of the oceans
and last survivor of the Titanic, auctions
possessions to pay nursing costs: a tiny brown
leather suitcase, squeezed full of clothes
which the people of New York pressed into
her small, cold fingers. Miss Millvina doesn't
look on the dark side, I mean not very often.
There's a saying: what can't be cured must be
endured. And she's the enduring kind. Behind
bottle-bottom specs she closes the afternoon clouds,
tilts her pale head, *I'm being very enduring*.